Thank Y(for This Day

Written by Crystal Bowman

Illustrated by Rusty Fletcher

This is the day that the Lord has made. Let us rejoice and be glad today! Psalm 118:24

For manufacturing information regarding this product, please call 1-800-323-9400.

ISBN 978-1-4143-9486-2

Printed in the United States of America

21	20	19	18	17	16	15
7	6	5	4	3	2	1

Tyndale House Publishers, Inc.
Carol Stream, Illinois

Wake up, Kitty!
Here comes the sun.

It's time to play
and jump and run.

No no, Kitty! Do not fight.
Let's play nice and do what's right.

Love your sisters and your brothers.
Kitties must be kind to others.

Brother's playing hide-and-seek.
Close your eyes and do not peek!

Kitty's looking here and there.
Kitty's looking everywhere!

Come back, Kitty. Don't you stray!
It's not safe to go that way.

Brother shares his tuna fish.
Kitty likes this tasty dish.

Uh-oh, Kitty! Are you hurt?
No—it's just a little dirt.

Do not worry. It's okay.
Mama cleans the dirt away.

Kitty shares a bedtime treat.
Creamy milk that's cool and sweet.

Kitties are all washed and fed.
Now it's time to go to bed.

Kitty shuts her eyes to pray,
"Thank you for a happy day."

"Thank you, God, for morning sun.
Thank you for a day of fun."

"Thank you for the moon so bright.
Thank you for a sleepy night. Amen."